Civil PE Practice Exam Transportation Depth: First Edition

Front cover image by Path to PE Services

Printed in the USA

Have a question? Reach out to pathtopeservices@gmail.com

About the Author

I wrote this book to help prospective Professional Engineers pass the NCEES Transportation Depth Exam. While studying, I struggled to find quality practice exams for the depth section, so I put this exam together shortly after becoming a Professional Engineer. I currently work for a mid-sized engineering consulting firm in the Baltimore-Washington Metropolitan region with a focus on transportation. I hope you find value in this publication and wish you the best of luck on exam day!

How to use this practice exam:

1. Tear/cut out the "scantron" provided on the next page.
2. Schedule 4 hours to take this exam with all the resources you plan on bringing on test day. The solution manual uses the Design Standards outlined by NCEES dated for exams beginning in April 2020.
3. Be sure to use an approved calculator, I prefer the TI-36X, as it has a useful solver function.
4. Try to simulate the testing environment as best you can and avoid using any electronic devices.
5. Once complete, check your answers against the key and solution manual and adjust your studying according. Aim for at least 28 correct answers.

Answer Sheet

1	Ⓐ Ⓑ Ⓒ Ⓓ	21	Ⓐ Ⓑ Ⓒ Ⓓ
2	Ⓐ Ⓑ Ⓒ Ⓓ	22	Ⓐ Ⓑ Ⓒ Ⓓ
3	Ⓐ Ⓑ Ⓒ Ⓓ	23	Ⓐ Ⓑ Ⓒ Ⓓ
4	Ⓐ Ⓑ Ⓒ Ⓓ	24	Ⓐ Ⓑ Ⓒ Ⓓ
5	Ⓐ Ⓑ Ⓒ Ⓓ	25	Ⓐ Ⓑ Ⓒ Ⓓ
6	Ⓐ Ⓑ Ⓒ Ⓓ	26	Ⓐ Ⓑ Ⓒ Ⓓ
7	Ⓐ Ⓑ Ⓒ Ⓓ	27	Ⓐ Ⓑ Ⓒ Ⓓ
8	Ⓐ Ⓑ Ⓒ Ⓓ	28	Ⓐ Ⓑ Ⓒ Ⓓ
9	Ⓐ Ⓑ Ⓒ Ⓓ	29	Ⓐ Ⓑ Ⓒ Ⓓ
10	Ⓐ Ⓑ Ⓒ Ⓓ	30	Ⓐ Ⓑ Ⓒ Ⓓ
11	Ⓐ Ⓑ Ⓒ Ⓓ	31	Ⓐ Ⓑ Ⓒ Ⓓ
12	Ⓐ Ⓑ Ⓒ Ⓓ	32	Ⓐ Ⓑ Ⓒ Ⓓ
13	Ⓐ Ⓑ Ⓒ Ⓓ	33	Ⓐ Ⓑ Ⓒ Ⓓ
14	Ⓐ Ⓑ Ⓒ Ⓓ	34	Ⓐ Ⓑ Ⓒ Ⓓ
15	Ⓐ Ⓑ Ⓒ Ⓓ	35	Ⓐ Ⓑ Ⓒ Ⓓ
16	Ⓐ Ⓑ Ⓒ Ⓓ	36	Ⓐ Ⓑ Ⓒ Ⓓ
17	Ⓐ Ⓑ Ⓒ Ⓓ	37	Ⓐ Ⓑ Ⓒ Ⓓ
18	Ⓐ Ⓑ Ⓒ Ⓓ	38	Ⓐ Ⓑ Ⓒ Ⓓ
19	Ⓐ Ⓑ Ⓒ Ⓓ	39	Ⓐ Ⓑ Ⓒ Ⓓ
20	Ⓐ Ⓑ Ⓒ Ⓓ	40	Ⓐ Ⓑ Ⓒ Ⓓ

1. A development is being planned at the location shown in the figure below. A traffic impact study is being conducted to assess the impact the development will have on the intersection of First St and Main St. The following information was collected:

- The development will generate 200 trips with 66% entering and 34% exiting along Main St.
- 50% of the new trips originate from the West, 50% from the East
- The distribution for the exiting trips is 30% Eastbound and 70% Westbound

The number of additional vehicles that will enter the study intersection is most nearly:

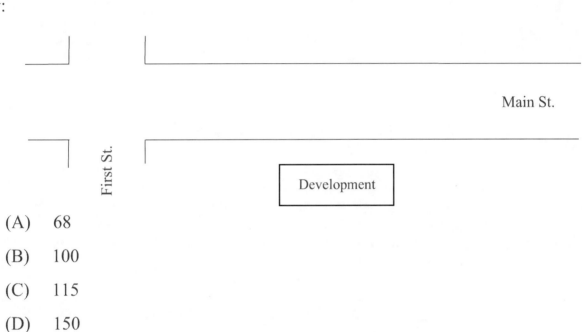

N

Main St.

First St.

Development

(A) 68

(B) 100

(C) 115

(D) 150

2. To meet minimum visibility requirements, how many signal faces should be provided for the major through movement at a signalized intersection?

(A)   1

(B)   2

(C)   3

(D)   None of the above

3. A basic freeway segment is found to operate at a speed of 40 MPH with a flow rate of 990 pc/h/ln. The LOS along the freeway is most nearly:

(A)   A

(B)   B

(C)   C

(D)   E

4.   The following information is given for an urban street segment:
   - The segment is a four-lane divided roadway with a speed limit of 45 MPH.
   - Raised curbs are present along the entire segment.
   - The segment has many driveways with 40 access points per mile.
   - Signalized intersections are spaced 300 feet apart.

The free flow speed (MPH) along the segment is most nearly:

(A)   31.8

(B)   32.5

(C)   38.6

(D)   40.1

5. According to AASHTO, the portion of roadway that allows for the movement of through traffic is called:

    (A) Through Lane

    (B) Travel Lane

    (C) Traveled Way

    (D) Highway

6. The maximum grade (%) along a collector with rolling terrain in a rural area where the AADT is less than 2,000 veh/day and the design speed is 25 MPH is most nearly:

    (A) 7

    (B) 10

    (C) 11

    (D) 12

7. A 2.0 % grade intersects a 4.0 % downgrade at an elevation of 600 feet at station 8+00. The length of the vertical curve is 1,000 feet. The elevation of turning point along the curve is most nearly:

(A) 593

(B) 603

(C) 648

(D) 690

G1= 2.0 % G2=- 4.0 %

8.   A combination truck is attempting to make a left turn from a stop onto the major road. The conflicting roadway has two lanes in each direction with a center grass median. All lanes are 12 feet wide, and the median is 6 feet wide. The design speed of the major roadway is 60 MPH and the minor road has an approach grade of +5%. The intersection sight distance (feet) needed to safely make the left turn maneuver is most nearly:

(A)   1050

(B)   1107

(C)   1195

(D)   1205

9. The station of the point of tangency for the horizontal curve shown below is most nearly:

(A)   STA 343+95.2

(B)   STA 355+78.3

(C)   STA 365+18.6

(D)   STA 356+16.9

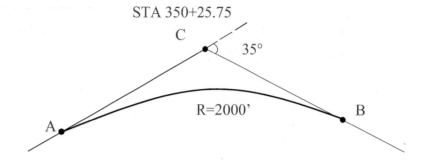

10. During the past 5 years an intersection had a total of 45 crashes. The local DOT determines that the crash rate for the intersection is 0.49 crashes per million entering vehicles (MEV). The average daily traffic (veh/day) entering the intersection is most nearly:

    (A)   50,000 veh/day

    (B)   55,000 veh/day

    (C)   85,000 veh/day

    (D)   95,000 veh/day

11. An existing signalized intersection has an average of 7.5 crashes per year. The intersection is in a suburban setting with two lanes in each direction. To reduce the number of crashes, a modern roundabout is proposed. The CMF for all crash severities is most nearly:

    (A)   0.99

    (B)   0.40

    (C)   0.52

    (D)   0.33

12. A new sidewalk is to be constructed in an urban setting where the clear width may be limited to a maximum of 4.5 feet. To meet ADA requirements, a passing space must be provided at a maximum interval of how many feet?

(A) 50

(B) 100

(C) 150

(D) 200

13. A straight two-lane highway that traverses in the East/West direction has an ADT of 800 vehicles per day and a design speed of 55 MPH. The lanes are 12 feet wide and the shoulders are 3 feet wide. The roadway traverses over a water way with a bridge that has the same lane and shoulder geometry. The embankment slope is 1V:5H. Tapered semi-rigid barriers are needed to protect the ends of the bridge and the waterway. Local policy requires the use of the maximum clear zone width. The barriers shall begin to taper 25 feet from the end of the bridge. The calculated barrier length-of-need (feet) for the Northeast approach to the bridge is most nearly:

(A) 105

(B) 108

(C) 110

(D) 112

14. Which of the following is not considered one of the steps in a traditional four step travel demand model?

    (A)   Mode Choice

    (B)   Trip Distribution

    (C)   Trip Assignment

    (D)   Time of day allocation

15. The stop line at a signalized intersection is located 50 feet horizontally from the signal indicators. The maximum height to the top of the signal housing above the pavement (feet) is most nearly:

    (A)   24.0

    (B)   24.5

    (C)   25.0

    (D)   25.6

16. The traffic volumes shown below were collected at a four way stop controlled intersection to assess the need for a traffic signal. All approaches are a single lane, and the major street has a posted speed limit of 35 MPH. Based exclusively upon the eight-hour vehicle volume warrant analysis under condition A, is the signal warranted?

    (A)   Yes, 8 hours met

    (B)   Yes, 9 hours met

    (C)   No, 3 hours met

    (D)   No, 6 hours met

Major Street Volumes

Hour Begins	NB	SB
6:00 AM	350	100
7:00 AM	370	150
8:00 AM	400	200
9:00 AM	410	190
10:00 AM	340	140
11:00 AM	300	75
12:00 PM	250	100
1:00 PM	200	210
2:00 PM	190	250
3:00 PM	200	330
4:00 PM	260	380
5:00 PM	250	450
6:00 PM	190	460

Minor Street Volumes

Hour Begins	EB	WB
6:00 AM	35	80
7:00 AM	45	190
8:00 AM	145	195
9:00 AM	175	150
10:00 AM	55	195
11:00 AM	35	160
12:00 PM	20	180
1:00 PM	40	110
2:00 PM	60	100
3:00 PM	45	140
4:00 PM	100	90
5:00 PM	120	95
6:00 PM	140	30

17. A shoulder along a two-lane highway needs to be closed temporarily to traffic. The posted speed limit along all the road is 40 MPH and the travel lanes are 12 feet wide. The shoulder is 9 feet wide. The length (feet) of the taper approaching the closed shoulder is most nearly:

(A)   80

(B)   110

(C)   240

(D)   320

18. The table below displays the total volume through two intersections in 15-minute intervals. The peak hour factor for the intersection with the most variability is most nearly:

   (A)   0.93

   (B)   0.95

   (C)   0.97

   (D)   0.99

Intersection 1

Time	Total Vehicles
3:00 to 3:15 pm	1506
3:15 to 3:30 pm	1672
3:30 to 3:45 pm	1701
3:45 to 4:00 pm	1695

Intersection 2

Time	Total Vehicles
3:00 to 3:15 pm	2122
3:15 to 3:30 pm	2322
3:30 to 3:45 pm	2532
3:45 to 4:00 pm	2411

19. A basic freeway segment has 5,000 vehicles in each direction per hour with 10-foot lanes and 6-foot shoulders. The terrain is level. The volume distribution includes 10.0% trucks and 3.0% recreational vehicles. The ramp density along the freeway is 4 ramps per mile and the PHF is 0.90 for both directions. To meet LOS E requirements for both directions, the total number of lanes needed across the freeway is most nearly:

(A)   2

(B)   4

(C)   6

(D)   8

20. If more than 20% of the pedestrians traveling along an urban sidewalk segment are elderly and the grade is greater than 10%, what average free flow walking speed (ft/s) should be used in the LOS methodology?

(A)   3.0

(B)   3.3

(C)   4.0

(D)   4.4

21. The phasing sequence that best describes the left turn phases along the Major Street in the ring and barrier diagram shown below is most nearly:

(A)   Split

(B)   Protected lead-lag

(C)   Protected lag-lag

(D)   Protected lead-lag and permitted

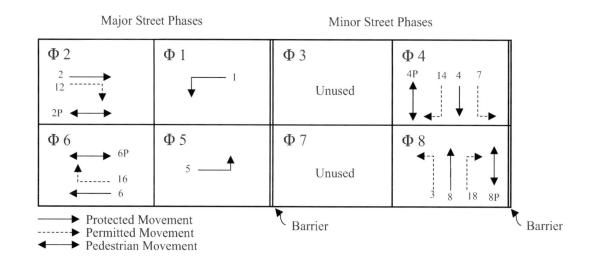

22.   A level 6-lane divided highway has a design speed of 75 MPH and a 15-foot
      median. The lanes are 12 feet wide, and the shoulders are 9 feet wide on the right
      side of the roadway. A section with a horizontal alignment has a radius of 2,000
      feet. If a wall is to be built along the roadway, how far from the centerline of the
      roadway should the wall be located (feet), to not obstruct the horizontal sight
      distance along the horizontal curve?

      (A)   41

      (B)   43

      (C)   80

      (D)   81

23.	A -2.0% grade intersects a 2.0% grade along a two-lane undivided roadway. The length of the curve is 750 feet. Based upon AASHTO criteria for headlight sight distance, what is the maximum design speed in MPH?

(A)	65

(B)	70

(C)	75

(D)	80

24.	A motorist is traveling at 45 MPH on a -1.5% grade when an animal suddenly enters the roadway. Assuming a reaction time of 2.5 seconds and a deceleration rate of 11.2 ft/sec^2, the distance (feet) the vehicle travels while braking before coming to a complete stop is most nearly:

(A)	200

(B)	300

(C)	370

(D)	410

25. A horizontal curve on a four-lane rural highway has the following characteristics:

Running Speed	55MPH
Coefficient of side friction	0.08
Radius at the point of intersection	1680 ft
Lane width	12 ft
Design ADT	15,000 vpd

The maximum superelevation allowed for this curve is most nearly:

(A) 1%

(B) 2%

(C) 6%

(D) 12%

26. A fixed object is to be shielded with a crash cushion along a freeway with a design speed of 70 MPH. For a preliminary design under unrestricted conditions, the minimum size of the crash cushion reserve area (ft^2) is most nearly:

   (A)   113

   (B)   248

   (C)   360

   (D)   392

27. According to AASHTO, which of the following is not a primary function of an island in an intersection setting?

   (A)   Division

   (B)   Channelization

   (C)   Refuge

   (D)   Storage

28. Which of the following is not a preventive treatment for jointed plain concrete pavement (JPCP)?

(A) Surface patches

(B) Edge Support

(C) Subsurface drainage

(D) Reseal joints

29. An excavation of a layered soil was conducted to maintain an underground pipe. Given the cross section and OHSA soil types below, the minimum horizontal distance X (feet) for the total width of the evacuation is most nearly:

(A) 10.5

(B) 21

(C) 23.5

(D) 26

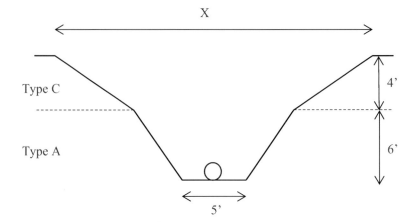

30. A spiral horizontal curve spans from STA 450+78 to STA 453+61 and has a rate of lateral acceleration of 1.45 ft/sec³. If the degree of curvature is 4.5°, the design speed (MPH) is most nearly:

(A) 50

(B) 55

(C) 60

(D) 65

31. A gravity model will be used to distribute trips to and from the zones found in the table below. The number of trips from zone 2 to 1 is most nearly:

(A) 146

(B) 280

(C) 1720

(D) 2870

Gravity Model: $T_{ij} = P_i (A_j F_{ij} / \sum A_j F_{ij})$

Zone	Production	Attraction	Trip Impedance between zones
1	3000	500	13
2	5000	4000	32
3	900	1500	59

32. A horizontal curve with a long chord of 1000 ft connects a tangent with a bearing of N 25° E to a tangent with a bearing of S 45° E. If the station Point of Intersection is 10+22, the station of the Point of Curvature is most nearly:

    (A)   1+50.27

    (B)   4+11.61

    (C)   3+22.01

    (D)   8+05.93

33. A traffic signal has a 180 second cycle length and an effective walk time of 32 seconds. The crosswalk is 9-feet-wide and 35 feet long and 25 pedestrians are waiting at the corner to cross the major street. If 19% of the pedestrians are elderly, the service time (sec) for pedestrians to cross the major street is most nearly:

    (A)   16.5

    (B)   17.5

    (C)   18.0

    (D)   19.0

34. A two-lane rural roadway has a vertical curve with the characteristics found in the table below. The minimum length (feet) of the vertical curve for stopping sight distance is most nearly:

(A)   450

(B)   525

(C)   575

(D)   605

G1	-2.0%
G2	3.0%
Design Speed	55 MPH
ADT	10,000

35. The number of conflict points at a four-leg single lane roundabout is most nearly:

(A)   4

(B)   8

(C)   16

(D)   32

36. A heavy truck is approaching a railroad crossing at a velocity of 45 MPH. A train approaching the crossing has a sight-distance of 990 feet along the railroad tracks. The grade crossing stop line is located 18 feet from the nearside rail and the truck driver is seated 9 feet back from the trucks front bumper. Utilizing AASHTO's standard values for brake-reaction time, the area (acre) of the triangle generated by the sight line for the truck to safely stop at the stop line is most nearly:

(A)   2

(B)   4

(C)   6

(D)   8

37. The flexible asphalt pavement cross section below is being designed for a roadway with an ESAL value of 1×10^6. The design serviceability loss is 0.05 and the overall standard deviation (S_o) is assumed to be 0.4. The reliability level (R) is assumed to be 85%. The structural number of the asphalt course is most nearly:

(A) 3

(B) 4

(C) 5

(D) 6

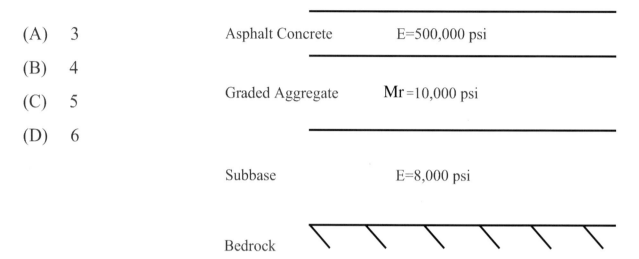

Asphalt Concrete	E=500,000 psi
Graded Aggregate	Mr =10,000 psi
Subbase	E=8,000 psi
Bedrock	

38. A unit hydrograph for an 800-acre watershed can be approximated by a triangular shape for a duration of 6 hours as shown below. The flow rate (acre-in/hr) at hour 2 is most nearly:

(A) 89

(B) 107

(C) 178

(D) 267

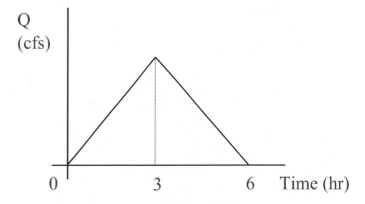

39. Two equally sized square concrete (n=0.01) box culverts are needed to collect runoff from a 10-acre area. The slope of both boxes is expected to be 2% and under full flow conditions, each culvert is expected to transfer 175 cfs. What is the minimum side length (feet) necessary for each pipe to convey the flow?

(A) 2.5

(B) 3.5

(C) 15.0

(D) 21.0

40. A contractor is in the market for a new tower crane and is considering the options listed in the table below. The interest rate is 10% and the expected life for each crane is 10 years. To minimize the cost, which crane should they choose and what is the capitalized cost?

	Crane 1	Crane 2
Purchase Price	$ 1,000,000	$ 1,500,000
Annual Revenue	$ 250,000	$ 350,000
Annual Operating Cost	$ 200,000	$ 150,000
Salvage Value	$ 300,000	$ 425,000

    (A)   Crane 1, $95,000

    (B)   Crane 1, $580,000

    (C)   Crane 2, $110,000

    (D)   Crane 2, $610,000

ANSWER KEY:

The following pages include a solution to each of the depth problems. The methodology and reference materials used are listed for your convenience. Please note that other approaches may be used to solve each problem.

During the actual PE Exam, I found it helpful to circle or underline the important information in the question. I also found it helpful to write the units needed in the answer at the top of each problem. If you find an error in any solution, please feel free to email us at pathtopeservices@gmail.com. If your looking for more practice problems, see our new "Civil PE Practice Exam: CBT transportation Depth" exam for more practice

Question	Answer
1	C
2	B
3	C
4	A
5	C
6	D
7	A
8	C
9	D
10	A
11	D
12	D
13	A
14	D
15	B
16	C
17	A
18	A
19	C
20	A

Question	Answer
21	C
22	D
23	B
24	A
25	D
26	B
27	D
28	A
29	D
30	B
31	A
32	A
33	D
34	C
35	B
36	B
37	B
38	C
39	B
40	C

1. A development is being planned at the location shown in the figure below. A traffic impact study is being conducted to assess the impact the development will have on the intersection of First St and Main St. The following information was collected:

- The development will generate 200 trips with 66% entering and 34% exiting along Main St.
- 50% of the new trips originate from the West, 50% from the East
- The distribution for the exiting trips is 30% Eastbound and 70% Westbound

The number of additional vehicles that will enter the study intersection is most nearly:

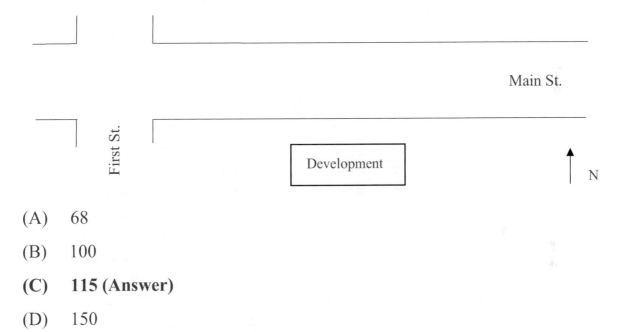

(A)   68

(B)   100

(C)   115 (Answer)

(D)   150

Solution:

1. Find the north arrow and calculate the number of trips generated by the development:

$$200 * 0.66 = 132 \; (Entering) \qquad 200 * 0.34 = 68 \; (Exiting)$$

2. Use bullet 2 to find where the trips come from (originate):

$$132 * 0.50 = 66 \; trips \; originate \; from \; the \; west \; and \; the \; east$$

3. Calculate the number of trips exiting Westbound and Eastbound:

$$0.7 * 68 = 47.6 \approx 48.0 \; new \; trips \; Westbound$$

$$0.3 * 68 = 20.4 \approx 20.0 \; New \; Trips \; Eastbound$$

4. Sum the total number of additional trips that travel through the study intersection, which is to the west of the development (remember to choose the answer that is <u>most nearly</u>):

$$66\ (entering\ trips\ from\ the\ West) + 48\ (westbound\ exiting\ trips) =$$
$$\mathbf{114\ (C)}$$

2.   To meet minimum visibility requirements, how many signal faces should be provided for the major through movement at a signalized intersection?

   (A)   1

   (B)   2 (Answer)

   (C)   3

   (D)   None of the above

Solution:

   1. The problem should point you towards the MUTCD.
   2. Refer to Page 459, section 4D.11.
      Part 01: "If a signalized through movement existing on an approach, a minimum of   **two (B)** primary signal face shall be provided for the through movement."

Material Referenced: Manual on Uniform Traffic Control Devices, 2009, including Revisions 1 and 2 dated May 2012, U.S. Department of Transportation—Federal Highway Administration, Washington, DC.

3.	A basic freeway segment is found to operate at a speed of 40 MPH with a flow rate of 990 pc/h/ln. The LOS along the freeway is most nearly:

(A)	A

(B)	B

**(C)	C (Answer)**

(D)	E

Solution:

1. The question asks for Level of Service (LOS), so you need to find your Highway Capacity Manual. The problem refers to a freeway segment, so you will need the uninterrupted flow section of the manual (Volume 2).
2. Refer to Chapter 12, Exhibit 12-16. With a flow rate of 990 pc/h/ln and a speed of 40 MPH, the density (pc/mi/ln) is between 18 and 26, which would indicate a LOS of C.

Material Referenced: Highway Capacity Manual,6th edition, Transportation Research Board—National Research Council, Washington, DC.

4. The following information is given for an urban street segment:
- The segment is a four-lane divided roadway with a speed limit of 45 MPH.
- Raised curbs are present along the entire segment.
- The segment has many driveways with 40 access points per mile.
- Signalized intersections are spaced 300 feet apart.

The free flow speed (MPH) along the segment is most nearly:

(A)   31.8 (Answer)

(B)   32.5

(C)   38.6

(D)   40.1

Solution:

1. For this problem you will need chapter 18 of the Highway Capacity Manual, Volume 3, Interrupted flow, as the road type is an urban street segment.
2. Base free flow speed is calculated from equation 18-3 on Page 18-28.

$$S_{fo} = S_{calib} + S_0 + f_{cs} + f_A + f_{pk}$$

3. The information given in the problem should be used along with Exhibit 18-11 to solve the equation above.

$$S_{fo} = 0.0 + 46.8 + (-2.7) + (-1.6) + 0.0 = 42.5 \ MPH$$

4. The question asked for free flow speed, not base free flow speed. Refer to equation 18-5 on page 18-29 to solve for free flow speed. Signal spacing adjustment factor (f_L) can be solved for using equation 18-4.

$$S_f = S_{fo} * f_L$$

$$f_L = 1.02 - 4.7 * \frac{S_{fo} - 19.5}{\max(L_s, 400)} \leq 1.0$$

5. Solve for F_L and then solve for S_f.

$$f_L = 1.02 - 4.7 * \frac{42.5 - 19.5}{400} = 0.7497 \ \leq 1.0 \ Okay$$

$$S_f = 42.5 * 0.7497 = 31.86 \ MPH \ (\boldsymbol{A})$$

<u>Material Referenced</u>: Highway Capacity Manual, 6th edition, Transportation Research Board—National Research Council, Washington, DC.

5. According to AASHTO, the portion of roadway that allows for the movement of through traffic is called:

    (A)   Through Lane

    (B)   Travel Lane

    (C)   Traveled Way (Answer)

    (D)   Highway

Solution:

1. Refer to the AASHTO Green Book, Chapter 4, Cross-Section Elements, page 4-1.

   "Traveled Way – the portion of the roadway that allows for the movement of through traffic, including vehicles, transit and freight."

Material Referenced: A Policy on Geometric Design of Highways and Streets, 7th edition, 2018 (including October 2019 errata), American Association of State Highway & Transportation Officials, Washington, DC.

6. The maximum grade (%) along a collector with rolling terrain in a rural area where the AADT is less than 2,000 veh/day and the design speed is 25 MPH is most nearly:

(A) 7

(B) 10

(C) 11

(D) 12 (Answer)

Solution:

1. Refer to the AASHTO Green Book Chapter 6, Collector Roads and Streets, page 6-4, table 6-2.
2. The key to this question is to not only read the table, but also the note below the table. If the AADT is less than 2,000 veh/day, the maximum grade may be up to 2.0% steeper than the grades shown in the table.
3. Thus, the answer is 10.0 % + 2.0 % = 12.0 % **(D)**

<u>Material Referenced</u>: A Policy on Geometric Design of Highways and Streets, 7th edition, 2018 (including October 2019 errata), American Association of State Highway & Transportation Officials, Washington, DC.

7. A 2.0 % grade intersects a 4.0 % downgrade at an elevation of 600 feet at station 8+00. The length of the vertical curve is 1,000 feet. The elevation of turning point along the curve is most nearly:

(A) **593 (Answer)**

(B) 603

(C) 648

(D) 690

Solution:

1. Use the following useful equations:

$$R = \frac{G_2 - G_1}{L} = Rate\ of\ grade\ change$$

$$T_p = \frac{-G_1}{R} = Distance\ to\ turning\ point$$

$$Elevation = \frac{R}{2} * X^2 + G_1 * X + (PVC\ Elevation)$$

2. Solve:

$$R = \frac{-0.04 - 0.02}{1000} = -0.00006$$

$$T_p = \frac{-0.02}{-0.00006} = 333.33'$$

$$Elevation\ of\ PVC = 600 - \left(0.02 * \frac{1000}{2}\right) = 590.0'$$

$$Elevation\ of\ Turning\ Point$$

$$= \frac{-0.00006}{2} * 333.33^2 + 0.02 * 333.33 + 590.0 = 593.33'\ (\boldsymbol{A})$$

8. A combination truck is attempting to make a left turn from a stop onto the major road. The conflicting roadway has two lanes in each direction with a center grass median. All lanes are 12 feet wide, and the median is 6 feet wide. The design speed of the major roadway is 60 MPH and the minor road has an approach grade of +5%. The intersection sight distance (feet) needed to safely make the left turn maneuver is most nearly:

    (A)   1050

    (B)   1107

    (C)   1195 (Answer)

    (D)   1205

Solution:

1. Draw a sketch:

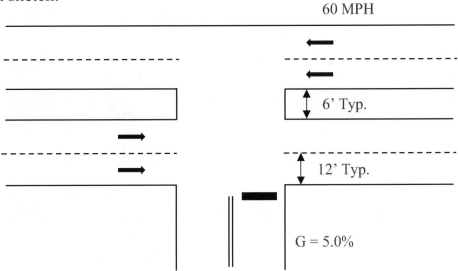

2. Refer to Case 1B in Section 9.5.3.2.1 of the AASHTO Green Book on pages 9-43 to 9-46. Intersection Sight Distance (ISD) is defined by equation 9-1.

$$ISD = 1.47 * V_{major} * t_g$$
$$V_{major} = Design\ Speed\ of\ Major\ Road\ (MPH)$$
$$t_g = Time\ gap\ for\ minor\ road\ vehicle\ to\ enter\ the\ major\ road$$

3. Use Table 9-6 on page 9-44 to find the time gap. For a combination truck making a left turn from a stop, 11.5 seconds are needed. Since the minor road's approach grade is 5.0%, 0.2 seconds need to be added for each percent grade greater than 0.0%. Also, since the left turn movement conflicts with 2 lanes, as well as one 6-

foot median, 0.7 seconds should be added to the time gap for each lane in excess of one. The median width should be converted to the equivalent number of lanes. Below describes the derivation of the total time gap:

$$Grade\ time\ gap\ adj. = 5 * 0.2 = 1.0\ seconds$$

$$Lanes\ time\ gap\ adj. = 0.7 + \left(\frac{0.7}{2}\right) = 1.05\ seconds$$

$$Total\ t_g = 11.5 + 1.0 + 1.05 = 13.55\ seconds$$

4. Solve for ISD:

$$ISD = 1.47 * 60 * 13.55 = 1195.11\ feet\ (\boldsymbol{C})$$

Material Referenced: A Policy on Geometric Design of Highways and Streets, 7th edition, 2018 (including October 2019 errata), American Association of State Highway & Transportation Officials, Washington, DC.

9. The station of the point of tangency for the horizontal curve shown below is most nearly:

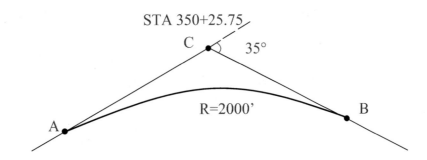

(A)   STA 343+95.2

(B)   STA 355+78.3

(C)   STA 365+18.6

(D)   STA 356+16.9 (Answer)

Solution:

1. Solve for the tangent length:

$$T = R * Tan\left(\frac{I}{2}\right) =$$
$$2000 * Tan\left(\frac{35}{2}\right) = 630.598'$$

2. Solve for the station of the Point of Curvature (PC):

$$PC = STA\ PI - T =$$
$$35025.75 + 630.598 = 34395.2' = STA\ 343 + 95.2$$

3. Solve for the length of the curve:

$$L = \frac{\pi * R * 35}{180} = \frac{\pi * 2000 * 35}{180} = 1221.73'$$

4. Solve for the station of the Point of Tangency (PT):

$$PT = STA\ PC + L =$$
$$34395.2 + 1221.73 = 35616.93' = STA\ 356 + 16.9\ (\boldsymbol{D})$$

10. During the past 5 years an intersection had a total of 45 crashes. The local DOT determines that the crash rate for the intersection is 0.49 crashes per million entering vehicles (MEV). The average daily traffic (veh/day) entering the intersection is most nearly:

    (A)   **50,000 veh/day (Answer)**

    (B)   55,000 veh/day

    (C)   85,000 veh/day

    (D)   95,000 veh/day

Solution:

1. Utilize the following equation, which can be derived from the given parameters in the problem's description:

$$Crash\ Rate\ (R)\ for\ an\ intersection = \frac{\#\ Crashes * 10^6}{365 * Time * Volume\ (ADT)}$$

2. Solve for ADT:

$$0.49 = \frac{45 * 10^6}{365 * 5 * ADT}$$
$$ADT = 50321.5\ (\boldsymbol{A})$$

11. An existing signalized intersection has an average of 7.5 crashes per year. The intersection is in a suburban setting with two lanes in each direction. To reduce the number of crashes, a modern roundabout is proposed. The CMF for all crash severities is most nearly:

(A)   0.99

(B)   0.40

(C)   0.52

(D)   0.33 (Answer)

Solution:

1. This question probes your capability to effectively use the Highway Safety Manual and tests your ability to find the correct information.
2. See Table 14-3 of the HSM on page 14-10.

Material Referenced: Highway Safety Manual, 1st edition, 2010, vols. 1–3 (including September 2010, February2012, and March 2016 errata), American Association of State Highway & Transportation Officials, Washington, DC.

12. A new sidewalk is to be constructed in an urban setting where the clear width may be limited to a maximum of 4.5 feet. To meet ADA requirements, a passing space must be provided at a maximum interval of how many feet?

(A) 50

(B) 100

(C) 150

(D) 200 (Answer)

Solution:

1. See page 74, section R302.4, "Passing Space" of the PROWAG.

"Where the clear width of pedestrian access routes is less than 5.0 feet, passing spaces shall be provided at intervals of 200 feet maximum."

Material Referenced: Proposed Accessibility Guidelines for Pedestrian Facilities in the Public Right-of-Way, July 26, 2011, and supplemental notice of February 13, 2013, United States Access Board, Washington, DC,www.access-board.gov.

13. A straight two-lane highway that traverses in the East/West direction has an ADT of 800 vehicles per day and a design speed of 55 MPH. The lanes are 12 feet wide and the shoulders are 3 feet wide. The roadway traverses over a water way with a bridge that has the same lane and shoulder geometry. The embankment slope is 1V:5H. Tapered semi-rigid barriers are needed to protect the ends of the bridge and the waterway. Local policy requires the use of the maximum clear zone width. The barriers shall begin to taper 25 feet from the end of the bridge. The calculated barrier length-of-need (feet) for the Northeast approach to the bridge is most nearly:

(A)   **105 (Answer)**

(B)   108

(C)   110

(D)   112

Solution:

1. This question gives you a lot 0f information in the problem statement, so stay organized and list what is given:
   - ADT = 800 vpd
   - Design Speed = 55 MPH
   - Lanes are 12 feet wide
   - Shoulders are 3 feet wide
   - Embankment slope 1 vertical to 5 horizontal
   - Tapered barriers
   - Maximum clear width
   - Taper begins 25 feet from the edge of the area to be protected.
   - Semi-Rigid Barrier

2. Draw a picture:

3. Refer to the Roadside Design Guide Page 5-51 for equation 5-1 to solve for X (length-of-need). Note that if a taper is not used, equation 5-2 should be used:

$$X = \frac{L_A + \left(\frac{b}{a}\right) * (L_1) - L_2}{\left(\frac{b}{a}\right) + \left(\frac{L_A}{L_R}\right)}$$

Where:

- L_A = Lateral extent of area of concern
- $\left(\frac{b}{a}\right)$ = Flare rate
- L_1 = Length of tangent barrier prior to taper
- L_2 = Lateral distance from the edge of the traveled way to the barrier
- L_R = Runout length = distance from the object being protected to the location where the vehicle departs from the traveled way

4. Use the following to solve the equation for the length-of-need:

- L_A = 24' = Clear zone width since the roadway is on an embankment and waterway extends beyond the clear zone (see page 5-49, second paragraph)
- $\left(\frac{b}{a}\right) = \frac{1}{12}$ Refer to page 5-48, Table 5-9. Remember to use column B for semi-rigid barrier systems
- L_1 = 25', given in problem statement
- L_2 = 3' for the Northeast quadrant
- L_R = 175, use interpolation from Table 5-10(b) on page 5-50

5. Solve:

$$X = \frac{24 + \left(\frac{1}{12}\right) * (25) - 3}{\left(\frac{1}{12}\right) + \left(\frac{24}{175}\right)} = 104.69 \approx 105' \ (\textbf{\textit{A}})$$

Material Referenced: Roadside Design Guide, 4thedition, 2011 (including February 2012 and July 2015 errata), American Association of State Highway & Transportation Officials, Washington, DC.

14. Which of the following is not considered one of the steps in a traditional four step travel demand model?

    (A)   Mode Choice

    (B)   Trip Distribution

    (C)   Trip Assignment

    (D)   Time of day allocation (Answer)

Solution:

1. The traditional four step travel demand model has the following steps:
   - Trip Generation
   - Trip Distribution
   - Mode Choice
   - Trip Assignment

15. The stop line at a signalized intersection is located 50 feet horizontally from the signal indicators. The maximum height to the top of the signal housing above the pavement (feet) is most nearly:

(A)   24.0

(B)   24.5 (Answer)

(C)   25.0

(D)   25.6

Solution:

1. Refer to the MUTCD, page 465, section 4D.15, figure 4D-5.

Material Referenced: Manual on Uniform Traffic Control Devices, 2009, including Revisions 1 and 2 dated May 2012, U.S. Department of Transportation—Federal Highway Administration, Washington, DC.

16. The traffic volumes shown below were collected at a four way stop controlled intersection to assess the need for a traffic signal. All approaches are a single lane, and the major street has a posted speed limit of 35 MPH. Based exclusively upon the eight-hour vehicle volume warrant analysis under condition A, is the signal warranted?

   (A)   Yes, 8 hours met

   (B)   Yes, 9 hours met

   (C)   No, 3 hours met (Answer)

   (D)   No, 6 hours met

Major Street Volumes

Hour Begins	NB	SB
6:00 AM	350	100
7:00 AM	370	150
8:00 AM	400	200
9:00 AM	410	190
10:00 AM	340	140
11:00 AM	300	75
12:00 PM	250	100
1:00 PM	200	210
2:00 PM	190	250
3:00 PM	200	330
4:00 PM	260	380
5:00 PM	250	450
6:00 PM	190	460

Minor Street Volumes

Hour Begins	EB	WB
6:00 AM	35	80
7:00 AM	45	190
8:00 AM	145	195
9:00 AM	175	150
10:00 AM	55	195
11:00 AM	35	160
12:00 PM	20	180
1:00 PM	40	110
2:00 PM	60	100
3:00 PM	45	140
4:00 PM	100	90
5:00 PM	120	95
6:00 PM	140	30

Solution:

1. Refer to section 4C.02 of the MUTCD page 437, which describes the eight hour vehicular volume. For the signal to be warranted under Condition A, the vehicles per hour given in both 100% columns in Table 4C-1 exist on the major street and the higher volume minor street approaches for each of any 8 hours. Importantly, the major street and minor street volumes should exceed the values in the 100% column for the same 8 hours.

2. The 70% column in Table 4C-1 cannot be used since the major street posted speed limit does not exceed 40 MPH.

3. For the warrant to be met, at least 500 vehicles per hour need to traverse along the major street at the intersection. Thus, the sum of the major street approach volumes must be greater than 500. Also, for the minor street, the higher-volume approach must exceed 150. The table below displays which hours were met:

Hour Begins	NB	SB	Total Volume
6:00 AM	350	100	450
7:00 AM	370	150	520
8:00 AM	400	200	600
9:00 AM	410	190	600
10:00 AM	340	140	480
11:00 AM	300	75	375
12:00 PM	250	100	350
1:00 PM	200	210	410
2:00 PM	190	250	440
3:00 PM	200	330	530
4:00 PM	260	380	640
5:00 PM	250	450	700
6:00 PM	190	460	650

Hour Begins	EB	WB
6:00 AM	35	80
7:00 AM	45	190
8:00 AM	145	195
9:00 AM	175	150
10:00 AM	55	195
11:00 AM	35	160
12:00 PM	20	180
1:00 PM	40	110
2:00 PM	60	100
3:00 PM	45	140
4:00 PM	100	90
5:00 PM	120	95
6:00 PM	140	30

4. For the Major Street, 7 hours were met. For the minor street 6 hours exceed the threshold. The only hours that meet both the criteria are 7AM, 8AM, and 9AM. So, the warrant is not met. The answer is **(C).**

Material Referenced: Manual on Uniform Traffic Control Devices, 2009, including Revisions 1 and 2 dated May 2012, U.S. Department of Transportation—Federal Highway Administration, Washington, DC.

17. A shoulder along a two-lane highway needs to be closed temporarily to traffic. The posted speed limit along all the road is 40 MPH and the travel lanes are 12 feet wide. The shoulder is 9 feet wide. The length (feet) of the taper approaching the closed shoulder is most nearly:

(A) **80 (Answer)**

(B) 110

(C) 240

(D) 320

Solution:

1. Utilize table 6H-4 on page 633 in the MUTCD to solve for the Taper Length (L):

$$L = \frac{W * S^2}{60} = \frac{9 * 40^2}{60} = 240'$$

2. Refer to Figure 6H-3 on page 639 to see that the taper length should be 1/3L.

$$\frac{240}{3} = 80' (A)$$

Material Referenced: Manual on Uniform Traffic Control Devices, 2009, including Revisions 1 and 2 dated May 2012, U.S. Department of Transportation—Federal Highway Administration, Washington, DC.

18. The table below displays the total volume through two intersections in 15-minute intervals. The peak hour factor for the intersection with the most variability is most nearly:

    (A)   **0.93 (Answer)**

    (B)   0.95

    (C)   0.97

    (D)   0.99

Intersection 1

Time	Total Vehicles
3:00 to 3:15 pm	1506
3:15 to 3:30 pm	1672
3:30 to 3:45 pm	1701
3:45 to 4:00 pm	1695

Intersection 2

Time	Total Vehicles
3:00 to 3:15 pm	2122
3:15 to 3:30 pm	2322
3:30 to 3:45 pm	2532
3:45 to 4:00 pm	2411

Solution:

1. To solve this problem, you must know the definition of the peak hour factor (PHF).

$$PHF = \frac{Total\ hourly\ volume}{Peak\ 15\ minute\ interval * 4}$$

2. Solve intersection 1:

$$PHF = \frac{6574}{1701 * 4} = 0.966$$

3. Solve intersection 2:

$$PHF = \frac{9387}{2532 * 4} = 0.927$$

4. A PHF of 1.0 indicates that the volume during each 15-minute interval is the same. Thus, with a lower PHF, more variable traffic flows can be expected.

19. A basic freeway segment has 5,000 vehicles in each direction per hour with 10-foot lanes and 6-foot shoulders. The terrain is level. The volume distribution includes 10.0% trucks and 3.0% recreational vehicles. The ramp density along the freeway is 4 ramps per mile and the PHF is 0.90 for both directions. To meet LOS E requirements for both directions, the total number of lanes needed across the freeway is most nearly:

(A) 2

(B) 4

(C) 6 (Answer)

(D) 8

Solution:

1. To find the total number of lanes (N), refer to the Highway Capacity Manual equation 12-23 on page 12-51:

$$N = \frac{V}{MSF_i * PHF * f_{HV}}$$

Where:
- MSF_i = Max Service Flow Rate
- PHF = Peak Hour Factor
- f_{HV} = Heavy Vehicle Factor
- V = Directional Daily Volume

2. Calculate the MSF by first finding the FFS (Free Flow Speed) from equation 12-2 on page 12-27:

$$FFS = BFFS - f_{LW} - f_{RLC} - 3.22 * TRD^{0.84}$$
$$FFS = 75.4 - 6.6 - 0 - 3.22 * 4^{0.84} = 58.48 \, MPH$$

3. Use Exhibit 12-37 on page 12-50 to select the MSF for LOS E. MSF = 2,300 pc/h/ln.

4. Solve for the Heavy Vehicle Factor f_{HV} using equation 12-10 on page 12-34:

$$f_{HV} = \frac{1}{1 + ((0.1 + 0.03) * (2 - 1))} = 0.8849$$

5. Solve for the number of lanes. Remember the question asked for the <u>total</u> number of lanes:

$$N = \frac{5000}{2300 * 0.9 * 0.8849} = 2.72 * 2 \approx 6.0 \text{ (C)}$$

<u>Material Referenced</u>: Highway Capacity Manual, 6th edition, Transportation Research Board—National Research Council, Washington, DC.

20. If more than 20% of the pedestrians traveling along an urban sidewalk segment are elderly and the grade is greater than 10%, what average free flow walking speed (ft/s) should be used in the LOS methodology?

    (A)   **3.0 (Answer)**

    (B)   3.3

    (C)   4.0

    (D)   4.4

Solution:

1. Refer to the Highway Capacity Manual page 18-48. Since the population of the pedestrians is more than 20% elderly, the walking speed of 3.3 ft/s is recommended. Also, since the grade is greater than 10%, the walking speed is reduced by 0.3 ft/s to 3.0 ft/s **(A)**.

<u>Material Referenced</u>: Highway Capacity Manual, 6th edition, Transportation Research Board—National Research Council, Washington, DC.

21. The phasing sequence that best describes the left turn phases along the Major Street in the ring and barrier diagram shown below is most nearly:

    (A)   Split

    (B)   Protected lead-lag

    (C)   Protected lag-lag (Answer)

    (D)   Protected lead-lag and permitted

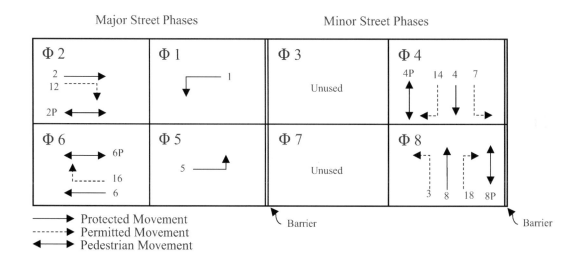

Solution:

    1. Refer to Exhibit 19-3 on page 19-8 of the Highway Capacity Manual.

<u>Material Referenced</u>: Highway Capacity Manual, 6th edition, Transportation Research Board—National Research Council, Washington, DC.

22. A level 6-lane divided highway has a design speed of 75 MPH and a 15-foot median. The lanes are 12 feet wide, and the shoulders are 9 feet wide on the right side of the roadway. A section with a horizontal alignment has a radius of 2,000 feet. If a wall is to be built along the roadway, how far from the centerline of the roadway should the wall be located (feet), to not obstruct the horizontal sight distance along the horizontal curve?

(A) 41

(B) 43

(C) 80

(D) 81 (Answer)

Solution:

1. Draw a sketch:

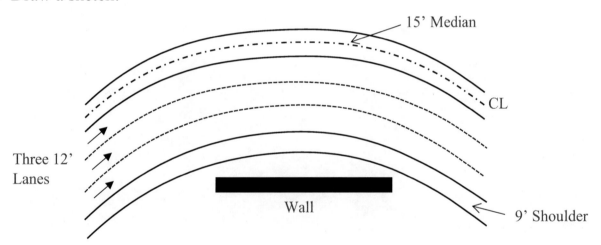

2. Use the AASHTO Green Book to determine the Stopping Sight Distance (SSD). From Table 3-1 on page 3-4, if the design speed is 75 MPH, then the SSD should be at least 820 feet.

3. Refer to equation 3-37 on page 3-115 to solve for the Horizontal sight line offset (HSO):

$$HSO = R * \left[1 - \cos\left(\frac{28.65 * S}{R}\right)\right]$$

4. Solve for the radius (R) for the centerline of the inside lane:
$$R = 2000 - 7.5 - (12 * 2) - 6 = 1962.5'$$

5. Solve for HSO:

$$HSO = 1962.5 * \left[1 - \cos\left(\frac{28.65 * 820}{1962.5}\right)\right] = 42.67'$$

6. The question asked for the distance from the centerline:

$$Distance = 7.5 + (12 * 2) + 6 + 42.67 = 80.17$$

7. The answer is **(D)** since 80.0' would not satisfy the HSO requirements.

Material Referenced: A Policy on Geometric Design of Highways and Streets, 7th edition, 2018 (including October 2019 errata), American Association of State Highway & Transportation Officials, Washington, DC.

23. A -2.0% grade intersects a 2.0% grade along a two-lane undivided roadway. The length of the curve is 750 feet. Based upon AASHTO criteria for headlight sight distance, what is the maximum design speed in MPH?

(A) 65

(B) 70 (Answer)

(C) 75

(D) 80

Solution:

1. First, realize the question is asking about a sag curve. Refer to the AASHTO Green Book, equation 3-49 and 3-50 on page 3-173 to solve for the light beam distance (S).

2. Using equation 3-49, solve for S (assuming S < L):

$$L = \frac{A * S^2}{400 + 3.5 * S}$$

Where:
- A = Algebraic difference in grades, percent
- S = Light beam distance, feet
- L = Length of the curve, feet

$$750 = \frac{|-2 - 2| * S^2}{400 + 3.5 * S}, \qquad S = 755.519'$$

Since S > L, equation 3-50 is used:

3. Solve for S:

$$L = 2 * S - \frac{400 + 3.5 * S}{A}$$

$$750 = 2 * S - \frac{400 + 3.5 * S}{4}, \qquad S = 755.55'$$

4. Now utilize Table 3-37 on page 3-176 to find the maximum design speed, which is 70 MPH **(B)**. If you chose (C), remember, the available headlight sight distance needed for the curve was determined to be 755 feet, if the design speed is 75 MPH, a vehicle would need 820 ft of light beam distance to stop.

Material Referenced: A Policy on Geometric Design of Highways and Streets, 7th edition, 2018 (including October 2019 errata), American Association of State Highway & Transportation Officials, Washington, DC.

24. A motorist is traveling at 45 MPH on a -1.5% grade when an animal suddenly enters the roadway. Assuming a reaction time of 2.5 seconds and a deceleration rate of 11.2 ft/sec², the distance (feet) the vehicle travels while braking before coming to a complete stop is most nearly:

(A) **200 (Answer)**

(B) 300

(C) 370

(D) 410

Solution:

1. Use the equation for braking distance below:

$$Braking\ Distance = \frac{V^2}{30 * (\frac{a}{32.2} \pm G)}$$

Where:
- V = Speed, MPH
- a = Acceleration/deceleration rate, ft/s²
- G = Grade, percent

$$Braking\ Distance = \frac{45^2}{30 * (\frac{11.2}{32.2} - 0.015)} = 202.8'\ (\textbf{A})$$

25. A horizontal curve on a four-lane rural highway has the following characteristics:

Running Speed	55MPH
Coefficient of side friction	0.08
Radius at the point of intersection	1680 ft
Lane width	12 ft
Design ADT	15,000 vpd

The maximum superelevation allowed for this curve is most nearly:

(A)   1%

(B)   2%

(C)   6%

(D)   12% (Answer)

Solution:

1. Refer to equation 3-11 on page 3-38 in the AASHTO Green Book. If your book does not have the same equation as below, be sure to check the Errata!

$$R_{PI} = \frac{V_R^2}{0.15 * e_{max}}$$

Where:
   - V_R = Running Speed, MPH
   - R_{PI} = Radius at the point of intersection
   - e_{max} = Maximum superelevation

2. Solve:

$$1680 = \frac{55^2}{0.15 * e_{max}}$$

$$e_{max} = 12.00 \% \text{ (D)}$$

<u>Material Referenced</u>: A Policy on Geometric Design of Highways and Streets, 7th edition, 2018 (including October 2019 errata), American Association of State Highway & Transportation Officials, Washington, DC.

26. A fixed object is to be shielded with a crash cushion along a freeway with a design speed of 70 MPH. For a preliminary design under unrestricted conditions, the minimum size of the crash cushion reserve area (ft²) is most nearly:

(A)   113

(B)   248 (Answer)

(C)   360

(D)   392

Solution:

1. Refer to Table 8-11 on page 4-46 of the Roadside Deign Guide. From the table, the dimension are below:
   - N = 8 ft
   - L = 45 ft
   - F = 3 ft

2. Now using the figure above Table 8-11, construct a diagram and solve for the area:

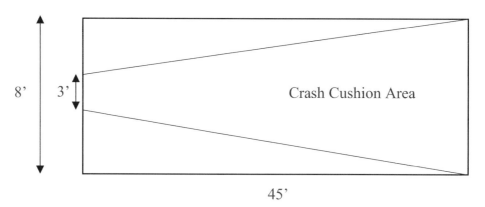

3. Solve for the area:

$$Area = (45 * 8) - [2 * (0.5 * 45 * 2.5)] = 247.5 \, ft^2 \, (\boldsymbol{B})$$

<u>Material Referenced</u>: Roadside Design Guide, 4thedition, 2011 (including February 2012 and July 2015 errata), American Association of State Highway & Transportation Officials, Washington, DC.

27. According to AASHTO, which of the following is not a primary function of an island in an intersection setting?

   (A)   Division

   (B)   Channelization

   (C)   Refuge

   (D)   Storage (Answer)

Solution:

1. Refer to page 9-69 on the AASHTO Green Book.

"Islands serve three primary function: (1) channelization – to control and direct traffic movement, usually turning; (2) division – to divide opposing or same direction traffic streams, usually through movements; and (3) refuge – to provide refuge for pedestrians and or bicyclists."

Material Referenced: A Policy on Geometric Design of Highways and Streets, 7th edition, 2018 (including October 2019 errata), American Association of State Highway & Transportation Officials, Washington, DC.

28. Which of the following is not a preventive treatment for jointed plain concrete pavement (JPCP)?

    (A) **Surface patches (Answer)**

    (B)   Edge Support

    (C)   Subsurface drainage

    (D)   Reseal joints

Solution:

1. Refer to Table 13-2 on page 149 of the Mechanistic-Empirical Pavement Design Guide (MEPDG). Surface patches are not a preventive treatment for the pavement type in question.

Material Referenced: Mechanistic-Empirical Pavement Design Guide: A Manual of Practice, 2nd edition, August2015, American Association of State Highway & Transportation Officials, Washington, DC

29. An excavation of a layered soil was conducted to maintain an underground pipe. Given the cross section and OHSA soil types below, the minimum horizontal distance X (feet) for the total width of the evacuation is most nearly:

(A)   10.5

(B)   21

(C)   23.5

(D)   26 (Answer)

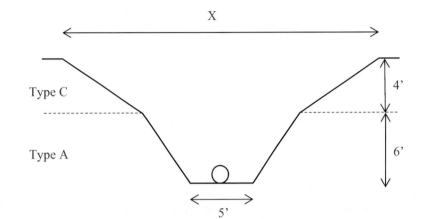

Solution:

1. The key to this problem is knowing the maximum allowable slope for the various types of OSHA soils. Refer to the OSHA's Construction Industry Regulations, or a general reference such as the Civil Engineering Reference Manual (Page 83-6, 16th edition). Below is a summary of the maximum allowable slope for each soil type:

- OSHA Type A- 3/4H:1V
- OSHA Type B- 1H:1V
- OHSA Type C- 1.5H:1V
- Stable Rock- Vertical

2. Solve for the "base" (horizontal component) of the Type A triangle:

$$6 * \frac{3}{4} = 4.5'$$

3. Solve for the "base" (horizontal component) of the Type C triangle:

$$4 * 1.5 = 6'$$

4. Solve for the total width:

$$(4.5 * 2) + (6 * 2) + 5 = 26' (D)$$

30. A spiral horizontal curve spans from STA 450+78 to STA 453+61 and has a rate of lateral acceleration of 1.45 ft/sec³. If the degree of curvature is 4.5°, the design speed (MPH) is most nearly:

(A) 50

(B) 55 (Answer)

(C) 60

(D) 65

Solution:

1. Solve for the length of the curve (L):

$$STA\ 450 + 78 = 45078'$$
$$STA\ 453 + 61 = 45361'$$
$$L = 45361 - 45075 = 286'$$

2. Use equation 3-26 in the AASHTO Green Book on page 3-74 to solve for speed (V):

$$L = \frac{3.15 * V^3}{R * C}$$

$$286 = \frac{3.15 * V^3}{R * 1.45}$$

Where: $R = \frac{5729.58}{4.5} = 1273.24'$

$$V = 54.94 \approx 55.0\ MPH\ (\boldsymbol{B})$$

Material Referenced: A Policy on Geometric Design of Highways and Streets, 7th edition, 2018 (including October 2019 errata), American Association of State Highway & Transportation Officials, Washington, DC.

31. A gravity model will be used to distribute trips to and from the zones found in the table below. The number of trips from zone 2 to 1 is most nearly:

Gravity Model: $T_{ij} = P_i (A_j F_{ij} / \sum A_j F_{ij})$

(A) **146 (Answer)**

(B) 280

(C) 1720

(D) 2870

Zone	Production	Attraction	Trip Impedance between zones
1	3000	500	13
2	5000	4000	32
3	900	1500	59

Solution:

1. Utilize the given gravity model to solve:

$$T_{21} = P_2 * \frac{A_1 * F_{21}}{(A_1 * F_{21}) + (A_2 * F_{12}) + (A_3 * F_{13})}$$

$$T_{21} = 5000 * \frac{500 * 13}{(500 * 13) + (4000 * 32) + (1500 * 59)} = 145.7 \ trips \ (A)$$

32. A horizontal curve with a long chord of 1000 ft connects a tangent with a bearing of N 25° E to a tangent with a bearing of S 45° E. If the station Point of Intersection is 10+22, the station of the Point of Curvature is most nearly:

    (A)   **1+50.27 (Answer)**

    (B)   4+11.61

    (C)   3+22.01

    (D)   8+05.93

Solution:

1. First, solve for the deflection angle (I) by drawing a picture:

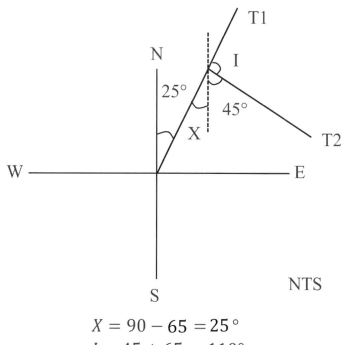

$$X = 90 - 65 = 25°$$
$$I = 45 + 65 = 110°$$

2. Use the following equation to solve for the tangent length (T):

$$T = \frac{LC}{2 * \cos\left(\frac{I}{2}\right)} =$$

$$T = \frac{1000}{2 * \cos\left(\frac{110}{2}\right)} = 871.72'$$

3. Solve for the station of the Point of Intersection (PI):

$$STA\ PC = STA\ PI - T = 1022 - 871.72 = 150.27 = STA\ 1 + 50.27\ (A)$$

33. A traffic signal has a 180 second cycle length and an effective walk time of 32 seconds. The crosswalk is 9-feet-wide and 35 feet long and 25 pedestrians are waiting at the corner to cross the major street. If 19% of the pedestrians are elderly, the service time (sec) for pedestrians to cross the major street is most nearly:

(A)   16.5

(B)   17.5

(C)   18.0

(D)   19.0 (Answer)

Solution:

1. Use equation 19-65 on page 19-82 of the Highway Capacity Manual to solve for the service time $(T_{ps,do})$.
2. Solve for $(T_{ps,do})$:

$$t_{ps,do} = 3.2 + \frac{L_d}{S_p} + 0.27 * N_{ped,do}$$

Where:

- $N_{ped,do}$ = Number of pedestrians waiting to cross the major street
- $g_{walk,mi}$ = Length of crosswalk "D", ft
- S_p = Pedestrian walking speed, ft/s

$$t_{ps,do} = 3.2 + \frac{35}{4.0} + 0.27 * 25.0 = 18.7 \; seconds \; (\boldsymbol{D})$$

<u>Material Referenced</u>: Highway Capacity Manual, 6th edition, Transportation Research Board—National Research Council, Washington, DC.

34. A two-lane rural roadway has a vertical curve with the characteristics found in the table below. The minimum length (feet) of the vertical curve for stopping sight distance is most nearly:

(A)   450

(B)   525

(C)   575 (Answer)

(D)   605

G1	-2.0%
G2	3.0%
Design Speed	55 MPH
ADT	10,000

Solution:

1. Solve for the algebraic difference in grades for the sag curve:

$$A = |3 - (-2)| = 5$$

2. Use Figure 3-37 on page 3-174 of the AASHTO Green Book to find the rate of vertical change (K).

$$K = 115$$

3. Solve for L:

$$K = \frac{L}{A}$$
$$115 = \frac{L}{5}$$
$$L = 575'(\boldsymbol{C})$$

<u>Material Referenced</u>: A Policy on Geometric Design of Highways and Streets, 7th edition, 2018 (including October 2019 errata), American Association of State Highway & Transportation Officials, Washington, DC.

35. The number of conflict points at a four-leg single lane roundabout is most nearly:

   (A)   4

   (B)   8 (Answer)

   (C)   16

   (D)   32

Solution:

1. There are 4 merging conflict points and 4 diverging conflict points for a total of 8 **(B)**. This contrasts to a conventional four leg signalized intersection with 32 conflict points.

36. A heavy truck is approaching a railroad crossing at a velocity of 45 MPH. A train approaching the crossing has a sight-distance of 990 feet along the railroad tracks. The grade crossing stop line is located 18 feet from the nearside rail and the truck driver is seated 9 feet back from the trucks front bumper. Utilizing AASHTO's standard values for brake-reaction time, the area (acre) of the triangle generated by the sight line for the truck to safely stop at the stop line is most nearly:

(A) 2

(B) 4 (Answer)

(C) 6 (Answer)

(D) 8

Solution:

1. The problem statement describes Case A for the sight distance at a rail crossing, where the vehicle operator can observe the approaching train in a sight line that will permit the vehicle to be brought to a stop prior to encroaching on the crossing area. Refer to pages 9-162 through 9-164 in the AASHTO Green Book.

2. The question is asking for the area of the triangle created by the sight line, similar to figure 9-67 on page 9-164. You must solve for the d_H leg of the triangle, as d_T was given as 990 ft:

$$d_H = (A * V_v * t) + \left(\frac{B * V_v^2}{a}\right) + (D) + (d_e)$$

Where d_H is the sight-distance along the highway for the truck to stop prior to encroaching on the crossing area in feet. Please refer to page 9-163 for the definition of each factor used above – most are constants.

3. Solve for d_H and the area:

$$d_H = (1.47 * 45 * 2.5) + \left(\frac{1.075 * 45^2}{11.2}\right) + (18) + (9) = 386.73'$$

$$Area = \frac{1}{2} * (386.73) * (990) = 191435.73 \ ft^2 * (2.29 * 10^{-5}) = 4.38 \ acre \ (\boldsymbol{B})$$

<u>Material Referenced</u>: A Policy on Geometric Design of Highways and Streets, 7th edition, 2018 (including October 2019 errata), American Association of State Highway & Transportation Officials, Washington, DC.

37. The flexible asphalt pavement cross section below is being designed for a roadway with an ESAL value of 1×10^6. The design serviceability loss is 0.05 and the overall standard deviation (S_o) is assumed to be 0.4. The reliability level (R) is assumed to be 85%. The structural number of the asphalt course is most nearly:

(A) 3

(B) 4 (Answer)

(C) 5

(D) 6

Asphalt Concrete	E=500,000 psi
Graded Aggregate	Mr=10,000 psi
Subbase	E=8,000 psi
Bedrock	

Solution:

1. Refer to the nomograph on page II-32 of the AASHTO Guide for Design of Pavement Structures to resolve the structural number. Be sure to use a straight edge!
2. The Mr value should be 10 ksi as it is the Effective Roadbed Soil Resilient Modulus."

Material Referenced: Guide for Design of Pavement Structures (GDPS-4-M), 1993, and 1998 supplement, American Association of State Highway & Transportation Officials, Washington, DC.

38. A unit hydrograph for an 800-acre watershed can be approximated by a triangular shape for a duration of 6 hours as shown below. The flow rate (acre-in/hr) at hour 2 is most nearly:

(A)   89

(B)   107

(C)   178 (Answer)

(D)   267

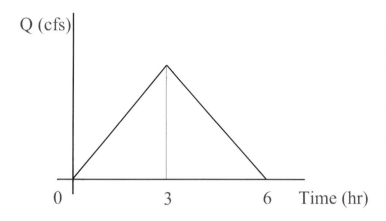

Solution:

1. A unit hydrograph is a graphical representation of the direct runoff from <u>one</u> unit of constant intensity rainfall over the watershed. Thus, the area under the unit hydrograph is the volume of runoff. The volume of runoff is 800 acre-in.

2. To solve for the flow rate (Q) at hour 2, you must first solve for the max flow rate, then solve for the slope along the line.

$$\frac{1}{2} * 6 * Q_{max} = 800$$
$$Q_{max} = 266.66 \; acre - in \; per \; hour$$

3. Solve for the slope of the line from hour 0 to hour 3.

$$Slope = \frac{(Y_2 - Y_1)}{(X_2 - X_1)} = \frac{266.66 - 0}{3 - 0} = 88.88$$

4. Solve for the flow rate at hour 2:

$$Q = 88.88 * (2) = 177.77 \; (C)$$

39. Two equally sized square concrete (n=0.01) box culverts are needed to collect runoff from a 10-acre area. The slope of both boxes is expected to be 2% and under full flow conditions, each culvert is expected to transfer 175 cfs. What is the minimum side length (feet) necessary for each pipe to convey the flow?

(A) 2.5

(B) 3.5 Answer

(C) 15.0

(D) 21.0

Solution:

1. Use Manning's equation to solve for the hydraulic radius of the culverts:

$$Q = \frac{1.49}{n} * A * R^{\frac{2}{3}} * \sqrt{s}$$

Where:
- Q = Flow rate
- n = Manning's roughness coefficient
- A = Cross sectional area of structure conveying flow,
  $X * X$ for a square
- $R^{2/3}$ = Hydraulic Radius,

$$R = (\frac{X^2}{4* X})^{2/3}$$

- s = Water surface slope
- X = Side width of box culvert

2. Solve for X:

$$175 = \frac{1.49}{0.01} * (X * X) * \left(\frac{X^2}{4* X}\right)^{\frac{2}{3}} * \sqrt{0.02}$$

$$X = 3.13 \text{ feet}$$

3. The answer is 3.5 ft (B).

40. A contractor is in the market for a new tower crane and is considering the options listed in the table below. The interest rate is 10% and the expected life for each crane is 10 years. To minimize the cost, which crane should they choose and what is the capitalized cost?

	Crane 1	Crane 2
Purchase Price	$ 1,000,000	$ 1,500,000
Annual Revenue	$ 250,000	$ 350,000
Annual Operating Cost	$ 200,000	$ 150,000
Salvage Value	$ 300,000	$ 425,000

(A) Crane 1, $95,000

(B) Crane 1, $580,000

(C) Crane 2, $110,000 (Answer)

(D) Crane 2, $610,000

Solution:

1. Draw the cash flow diagram for Crane 1, then solve for the capitalized cost:

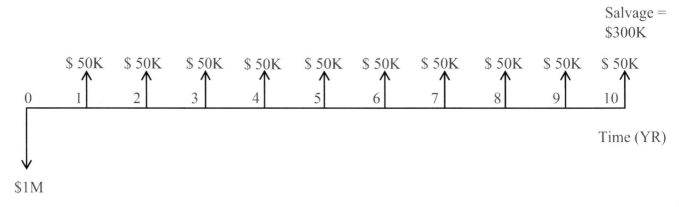

Where:

$$Annual\ Revenue\ C1 = \$250,000 - \$200,000 = \$50,000$$

2. Solve for the PW of Crane 1:

$$CC\ C1 = 1M - 50,000 * \left(^P/_A, i = 10\%, n = 10\right) - 300,000\left(^P/_F, i = 10\%, n = 10\right)$$
$$CC\ C1 = 1M - 50,000 * (6.1446) - 300,000 * (0.3855) = \$577,120.0$$

3. Draw the cash flow diagram for Crane 2, then solve for the present worth (PW):

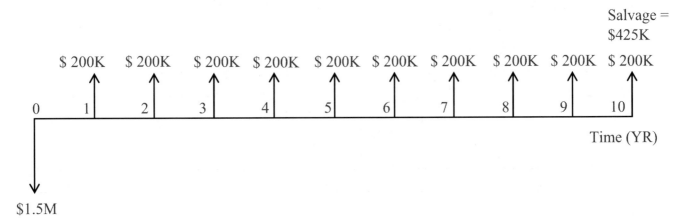

Where:

$$Annual\ Revenue\ C2 = \$350,000 - \$150,000 = \$200,000$$

4. Solve for the PW of Crane 2:

$$CC\ C2 = 1.5M - 200,000 * \left(\frac{P}{A}, i = 10\%, n = 10\right)$$
$$- 425,000\left(\frac{P}{F}, i = 10\%, n = 10\right)$$

$$CC\ C2 = 1.5M - 200,000 * (6.1446) - 425,000(0.3855) = \$107,242.5$$

5. Crane 2 has a capitalized cost of 107K while Crane 1 has a capitalized cost of 577K. Choose Crane 2 **(C)**.